DAMIAN

ACE DETECTIVE

THE CASE OF THE
POP STAR'S WEDDING

Written by Barbara Mitchelhill
Illustrated by Tony Ross

Published by Pearson Education Limited, Edinburgh Gate, Harlow, Essex, CM20 2JE.
Registered company number: 872828

www.pearsonschools.co.uk

Adapted text based on *Damian Drooth Supersleuth: The Case of the Pop Star's Wedding*, originally published by Andersen Press Limited in 2002.

Text © 2002 Barbara Mitchelhill

Illustrations © 2002 Tony Ross
Adaptation by Barbara Mitchelhill
Cover/interior illustrations and text all used by kind permission of Andersen Press Limited.

The right of Barbara Mitchelhill to be identified as the author of this work has been asserted by her in accordance with the Copyrights, Designs and Patents Act 1988.

First published 2012

15 14 13 12 11
10 9 8 7 6 5 4 3 2 1

British Library Cataloguing in Publication Data
A catalogue record for this book is available from the British Library.

ISBN 978 0 435 07587 3

Copyright notice

Printed in Malaysia (CTP-VP)

Acknowledgements
We would like to thank the children and teachers of Bangor Central Integrated Primary School, NI; Bishop Henderson C of E Primary School, Somerset; Brookside Community Primary School, Somerset; Cheddington Combined School, Buckinghamshire; Cofton Primary School, Birmingham; Dair House Independent School, Buckinghamshire; Deal Parochial School, Kent; Newbold Riverside Primary School, Rugby and Windmill Primary School, Oxford for their invaluable help in the development and trialling of the Bug Club resources.

Every effort has been made to contact copyright holders of material reproduced in this book. Any omissions will be rectified in subsequent printings if notice is given to the publishers.

CONTENTS

Chapter 1
An Amazing Invitation

My name is Drooth. Damian Drooth. Crime buster and ace detective.

Let me tell you about my latest case. It started when a letter arrived addressed to Mrs Drooth, Home Cooking Unlimited.

Dear Mrs Drooth,

I would love you to cook the food for my wedding.

Please could you come and discuss the menu?

Yours,

Tiger Lilly

I stared at the signature. I was gobsmacked.

"Is that Tiger Lilly the singer?" I yelled. *"One of the Bay Babes?"*

Mum nodded and my head exploded. I was Tiger Lilly's number one fan! Wow! Wow! Wow!

That morning, Mum telephoned Tiger Lilly and agreed to meet her.

"I'll come with you," I said.

"I don't think so," said Mum.

"You might get lost," I insisted.

"I can read a map, Damian."

"I could be your secretary and take notes."

"I don't want a secretary."

I tried something different.

"Right! I'll go on hunger strike if you don't take me!"

Mum sighed. "Don't be stupid, Damian! NO!"

In the end, she gave in. My mum's brain is no match for my cunning. I was going to meet the fabulous Tiger Lilly!

Chapter 2
I Meet Tiger Lilly

Tiger Lilly's house was mega huge! There she was, waiting on the steps for us. A proper star!

Then Mum spoke.

"This is my little boy, Damian," she said in her mumsy voice. "I couldn't leave him at home. He's always getting into trouble."

I ask you! Embarrassing or what? But I stuffed my hands in my pockets and just said, "Hi!" as if I met celebrities every day.

We followed Tiger Lilly down the hall and into a fantastic room with big comfy chairs.

"Well, Damian," she said, as she poured us some tea. "I've got a little brother and he's always in trouble, too!"

"It may seem like trouble to some," I said, darkly. "The fact is, I work undercover. Detective work."

I could see she was dead impressed.

"I track down crooks ... bank robbers ... forgers ... that kind of thing."

Tiger Lilly turned and looked at Mum.

"You didn't tell me your son was a detective!" she said. Then she winked – or maybe she had something in her eye. "Damian will be useful on the day of the wedding. I don't want my presents getting stolen, eh?"

Mum look horrified.

"Oh, Damian won't be here on your wedding day," she said. "I wouldn't want him here with all your guests around. He'll just get in the way."

What a cheek! After all the times I've helped her out! After all that washing up I've done!

Luckily, Tiger Lilly insisted I came. "You do the food, Mrs Drooth. Damian can keep a lookout for robbers."

Mum couldn't say anything then, could she? I had been employed as a private detective at the Wedding-of-the-Year. Yes!

Chapter 3
On Duty at the Wedding

Mum was in a real flap on the morning of the wedding. Me? I'd got my gear together – my notepad and my pen – and I was ready to fight any crime, big or small.

"Damian!" Mum shouted. "Don't just stand there. Help me get these puddings into the van."

I ask you! Does James Bond carry puddings for his mum? No! But that day, she was in a bit of a mood. So I did it.

I carried the chocolate mousse as carefully as I could. Was it my fault if the path was uneven? Was it my fault if I slipped?

Mum didn't speak to me all the way to Tiger Lilly's place. She just gripped the steering wheel and frowned at the road ahead.

When we reached the house, there was a security man on the gate. He was huge and wore a badge with DEAN on it. I must say, I was surprised that Tiger Lilly had employed him when she knew I was coming.

Mum stopped and wound down the window.

"I need to see your passes," said Dean.

Mum handed her card out of the window. I leaned over and flashed the detective badge I had made the night before. It was very impressive and we were waved straight in. No problem.

The lawn in front of Tiger Lilly's house was filled with an enormous tent (called a *marquee*). There were loads of people carrying chairs and arranging flowers. Mum parked the van behind the marquee and started unloading the food. She was dashing backwards and forwards like a wild thing.

I offered to help but she said she'd
rather do it herself.

"All right," I said. "I'll go and look
for criminals."

Mum gave me one of her looks.
"Don't you dare get into trouble!"
she yelled over a pile of sandwiches.
"I've got enough to do without
worrying about you."

"Stay cool!" I said. "I'm in control." Then I put on my shades and walked away.

It wasn't long before I saw a man who was dead suspicious. He was wearing a black suit with a white shirt and was carrying a black leather case. Worst of all he had a beard. He looked very suspicious. I did a quick sketch of him in my notebook. Then I followed him into the house. It was obvious he was planning to steal the wedding presents. That wasn't going to happen while I was on duty.

Chapter 4
I Spot a Criminal

I walked behind the man with my
back pressed against the wall, just
like a TV detective. But, before I got
close, somebody shouted, "Hey, kid!
What do you think you're doing?"

A security guard grabbed me by
·the collar.

I checked his name badge (which
said CURT) and showed him mine.

"I'm Tiger Lilly's personal protection officer," I told him.

Curt laughed! What was so funny?

"Out you go, sonny," he said. "Go and find your mum."

Of course, I did no such thing. When Curt had gone, I hurried back towards the house to watch over Tiger Lilly's presents.

As I peeped through the window, I saw them all spread out on a table.

In the very middle was a fantastic diamond necklace with a large label that said:

To Tiger Lilly on our wedding day.

From Gary, with love and kisses.

YUK!

Tiger Lilly was marrying Gary Blaze. I didn't know why. He was a footballer with skinny legs and no hair. He was useless at everything except scoring goals. What she needed was a guy with laser brainpower like me.

As I looked through the window, I saw the man with the beard walk into the room. He was staring at the diamond necklace. I could tell he was going to steal it when Curt wasn't looking.

I ran to the front door and hid behind the ivy, waiting for the bearded man to come out. When he did, I followed him down the path.

Then suddenly he looked at his watch and started running towards the marquee. He lifted a loose flap at the back of the tent and sneaked inside. Suspicious or what? But I was onto him.

By that time, the wedding reception was in full swing. Everybody was eating and talking. I hurried round to the main entrance. I could see Tiger Lilly in a long white dress with flowers in her hair and silver nail varnish. She looked fantastic! Gary Blaze looked stupid in a blue suit.

I looked round trying to spot the thief. YES! There he was, hiding amongst the band. Very clever, I don't think.

If he thought he would get away with that necklace – he was making a *big mistake*!

Chapter 5
Trapped in the Van

I ran towards Tiger Lilly to tell her what was going on. But, before I could get near, a hand landed on my shoulder. A security guard called KELVIN dragged me outside. "What do you think you're playing at?" he said.

I started to explain. "I'm tracking down ..."

Before I could finish, Curt came dashing out of the big house shouting, "Come quick, Kelvin!"

Kelvin dropped me like a hot potato and ran. I followed, of course. I could tell something was up.

"The diamond necklace has been nicked," said Curt.

"I know that already," I said – just to be helpful.

The guards turned and stared at me.

"How do you know that?" asked Kelvin.

"I'm a Private Detective," I replied, holding out my badge.

They raised their eyebrows and smirked. I ignored the smirk and carried on.

"I saw a man take the necklace."

(It was *nearly* true. I *almost* saw him.)

"He was a tall and thin with a beard, wearing a black suit, a white shirt and carrying a black case."

They looked at me as if I'd crawled out from under a stone.

"That's Dave," said Curt. "He plays in the band."

"No!" I said. "That's just a cover. He's really a thief."

They snorted and pushed me to one side.

"Ring the police, Curt," said Kelvin. "I'll put this boy where he can't get into trouble."

Kelvin didn't let me explain. He slung me over his shoulder like a sack of carrots. Then he carried me to Mum's van. What a cheek!

"Right!" he said as he flung me into the back. "You can stay there until your mum's finished with the food. Then she can deal with you." Then he slammed the door shut.

Suddenly I felt weak. It was the stress of chasing criminals – and lack of food.

Luckily, there was a chocolate gateau in the back of the van. My favourite! So I had a slice – and another – then another. It was in the interest of crime detection.

REMEMBER THIS TIP: Chocolate gateau is excellent for energy.

Now I was ready for action. Escaping would be no problem. The lock on the van door was broken. But the guard didn't know that, did he? He thought he'd locked me in. Tee hee!

Slowly, I opened the door and peeped out. I was a few metres from the entrance of the marquee.

I could see Tiger Lilly (still looking fantastic) and the band on the far side. There were security guards everywhere. It was almost impossible to get into the marquee without being seen. How could I reach the thief and save the diamond necklace?

Chapter 6
Gotcha!

Being a trained detective, I soon had the problem sorted.

Between the van and the entrance to the marquee was a large trolley with the wedding cake on top. Perfect! A waiter stood near the trolley. He was old and wrinkled – he must have been at least forty.

"Excuse me!" I called to him and pointed. "Somebody's looking for you. I can hear them shouting over there."

The waiter went off round the
back of the van. That was my
chance. I ran to the trolley, lifted the
cloth and climbed onto the bottom
shelf.

The waiter was back in no time.

"Young 'uns!" I heard him mutter.
"Up to their tricks again!"

Then he pushed the trolley into
the marquee with me on board. He
stopped in front of the bride's table.
Everybody cheered as Tiger Lilly and
the bald footballer walked towards
the cake ready to cut it.

That's when I leapt out.

"HOLD EVERYTHING!" I shouted. "STAND CLEAR!" I added. "THERE IS A CROOK IN HERE AND HE'S STOLEN A DIAMOND NECKLACE!"

The security guards came running towards me from every corner of the tent.

I jumped back onto the trolley and pushed off with one foot, skimming over the floor towards the band.

"IT'S HIM!" I shouted, pointing ahead. "IT'S THE ONE WITH THE SAXOPHONE! HE STOLE THE NECKLACE! IT'S IN HIS CASE!"

By then, the trolley was out of control and it smashed into the band. The cake shot across the floor leaving a lake of white icing and cream behind it, while I whizzed through the air like Superman and landed on the stage.

"GOTCHA!" I said, as I stared
up into the face of the man with the
beard. But he didn't move. I couldn't
understand it.

Then the man *behind* him
suddenly leapt off the stage and
made a run for it.

He skidded on a splodge of cream and his feet flew out from under him. He crashed onto his back like a beached whale.

He must be up to no good, I thought to myself. I grabbed his case and there inside it was the diamond necklace.

"I think he's forgotten something," I shouted, holding the necklace up for all to see.

Everybody was on their feet. They stood in a great circle round the crook, to get a better look.

In the middle of all this excitement, the police arrived.

"What's going on?" said the Inspector. "Have you caught the thief?"

"Thanks to this boy, we have," said Tiger Lilly. "This is Damian Drooth and he could teach the police a thing or two about solving crimes."

As she spoke, she put her arm round my shoulder. I almost fainted with pride.

Chapter 7
A Lucky Mistake!

Although I am brilliant at solving crimes, in this case I made a bit of a mistake. You see, I was never any good at music. So when I shouted, "It's the one with the saxophone!" and pointed at the band, I got it wrong. The man with the beard was playing a trumpet.

For your information, this is a trumpet …

This is a saxophone.

Just as well I got it wrong
because the *real* thief was playing
a saxophone. He thought I was
pointing at him. No wonder he ran.

Tiger Lilly was thrilled I'd foiled
the crook. "Oh Damian," she said,
"You are so clever. I'll give you a set
of all my CDs." Then she kissed me
on the cheek.
That was a bit
girlie for me
but it was
OK, really.

Gary Blaze went all smarmy and said, "Thanks, Damian." He wanted to give me a football and sign it, but I said, "No thanks. I'm not keen on football." That told him.

Everybody cheered me and made a great fuss. Kelvin even brought me two plates of food, and said, "Sorry, Damian. We've run out of chocolate gateau."

I didn't tell him I'd already had some.

I thought it best not to.